RAILWAYS OF CUMBRIA

PATRICK BENNETT

AMBERLEY

First published 2022

Amberley Publishing
The Hill, Stroud
Gloucestershire, GL5 4EP

www.amberley-books.com

Copyright © Patrick Bennett, 2022

The right of Patrick Bennett to be identified as
the Author of this work has been asserted in
accordance with the Copyrights, Designs and
Patents Act 1988.

ISBN 978 1 3981 0918 6 (print)
ISBN 978 1 3981 0919 3 (ebook)

British Library Cataloguing in Publication Data.
A catalogue record for this book is available from
the British Library.

Origination by Amberley Publishing.
Printed in the UK.

Introduction

There is surely no other region of Britain that can show such an extraordinary variety of railways as can the area we now know as Cumbria. No less than sixteen pre-grouping companies are represented within its borders, seven of these in Carlisle alone. The region is dominated by the mountains and lakes of the Lake District. To the east are the great Anglo-Scottish lines of the London & North Western and the Midland, not forgetting the thwarted ambition of the 'Little North Western'. Venturing across the Pennines were the transversal routes of the North Eastern Railway, from Newcastle to Carlisle, and Darlington to Tebay and Penrith.

The Cumbrian coast presents a completely different picture. Here the multiple competing companies were concerned principally with the transport of coal and mineral ores to serve the huge industrial complexes to the west and south. Transport of passengers to the Irish Sea ports was also important. The two principal coastal lines were the Maryport & Carlisle in the north and the Furness in the west and south. In the Whitehaven/Workington hinterland were a number of competing railways, all concerned with mineral extraction and transport.

A number of lines penetrated into the interior of the upland area. These were the Coniston, Lakeside and Windermere branches and the Cockermouth, Keswick & Penrith Railway, which crossed the Lake District from west to east. In the north two Scottish companies had lines in England. These were the Caledonian with its main line to Carlisle and the short-lived Solway Junction Railway; and the North British with the Waverley, Port Carlisle, and Silloth lines. The Glasgow and South Western also ran trains into Glasgow. The history, development, and in some cases closure, of each of these lines is described in turn, illustrated with a selection of photographs from different periods in their history.

CUMBRIA
SELECTED STATIONS

NB
Langholm
Lockerbie
Kershopefoot
CAL
Dumfries
Kirtlebridge
Riddings
Annan   GSW   Longtown
NER
Denton Village   Haltwhistle
Bowness   Port Carlisle   Rockcliffe   Milton
Bampton Jcn   Lambley
Kirkbride
CARLISLE
Silloth   Dalston
Abbeyholme
Black Dyke   See map p. 66
M&C
Wigton   Armathwaite   Alston
Brayton   LNW
Bulgill Aspatria   MR
Mealsgate
Maryport   Cockermouth
Workington   Bassenthwaite Lake
Penrith   Culgaith
CK&P   Troutbeck
Keswick   Clifton   Cliburn
Whitehaven   Kelton   Threlkeld   Appleby
Fell
See map p.xx   Shap
Gaisgill   Kirkby
Beckermet   Stephen
Sellafield   Tebay   Ravenstonedale
Seascale Boot
Drigg R&E   Coniston   Windermere
Ravenglass   Low Gill
&Eskdale   Torver   Sedbergh   Garsdale
Bootle   Oxenholme
FR Millom   Woodland   Barbon   Dent
Foxfield   Lakeside
Greenodd Haverthwaite Heversham   Ribblehead
Ulverston Arnside
Askam   Grange   Burton &   Kirkby
Holme   Lonsdale
Lindal   Kent's Bank   Arkholme   Horton
BARROW   Ingleton
CARNFORTH
Piel   Wennington

The railways of Cumbria.

The Newcastle & Carlisle Railway

The first railway to reach Carlisle was the Newcastle & Carlisle. It received its Act on 22 May 1829 and the first section between Hexham and Blaydon was completed by 9 March 1835. There was a slight problem in that the Act forbade the use of steam engines, a matter that was not resolved until 17 June. The line between Carlisle and Greenhead was opened on 19 July 1836, with an extension to the canal basin opening on 9 March 1837. The line was open in its entirety on 18 June 1838. In Cumbria there were stations at Scotby, Wetheral, Heads Nook, How Mill, Milton (later Brampton), Naworth and Low Row. Of these only Wetheral and Brampton remain open, the remainder having closed at various dates in the 1950s and 1960s. The original N&C station in Carlisle was at London Road, which closed in 1863, after which services terminated at Carlisle Citadel. Passing Brampton Fell signal box on 29 August 1991 is unit No. 156463 with a service for Newcastle.

Not far away is Milton signal box, an NER type N2 box constructed in 1893. Brampton station lies between these two signal boxes.

The Brampton Railway

A wagonway had existed since the late eighteenth century bringing coal from Tindale Fell to Brampton. This line crossed the N&C at Milton. With the arrival of the N&C it was decided to divert the wagonway to connect with it at Brampton Junction. Soon after, locomotive haulage was instituted, one of the locomotives used briefly being *Rocket* of Rainhill fame. Subsequently the Brampton Railway acquired its own locomotives, some being built in the company's workshops. The railway had numerous branches to various collieries and quarries and extended as far as Midgeholme. In 1851 the Alston branch opened and a line was built from Lambley to Lambley Colliery. The Brampton railway was extended from Midgeholme to meet this line, thus giving a through route from Brampton to Lambley. A horse-drawn passenger service between Brampton Junction and Brampton Town existed between 1836 and 1881. In 1913 the NER took over the line and started a locomotive-hauled service. This did not last long, being withdrawn in 1923. The locomotive is *Dandie Dimont*, one of the engines used on the Brampton Railway.

The Alston Branch

The N&C's original plan was a line from Haltwhistle to Nenthead, the Act for which was received on 26 August 1846. However, economic circumstances meant that the projected line beyond Alston had to be abandoned. The new Act, which now included a branch from Lambley to the Brampton Railway at Halton Lea Gate, was passed on 13 July 1849. The 13-mile line was opened throughout on 17 November 1852. The line followed the valley of the River South Tyne, which it crossed several times, and had gradients as steep as 1 in 56 and 1 in 70. There were stations at Featherstone Park, Coanwood, Lambley, Slaggyford, and Alston. A splendid view of the station yard at Alston taken in 1954. (Photo: Walter Dendy)

On the same day a Standard Class 3MT 2-6-0 waits to leave Alston for Haltwhistle. (Photo: Walter Dendy)

An initial timetable saw two daily trains each way on weekdays. By 1895 there were four, with a journey time of thirty-five minutes. By 1947 this had grown to seven with an additional service on Saturdays. Journey time had speeded up by one minute! A similar timetable was operating at the time of closure with most services in the hands of Class 101 Metro-Cammell units. The line survived as long as it did only because there was no all-weather road to Alston. Once this was built the line's days were numbered and the last train ran on 1 May 1976. In 1973 a group of ramblers await the arrival of a Metro-Cammell DMU at a much reduced Alston station. (Photo: John Ragla)

Before the railway closed the South Tynedale Railway Society tried to raise the money to purchase the line from BR. Sadly their attempt failed and the track was removed. However, all was not lost and in 1983 the STRPS opened a 2-foot gauge tourist railway, which has been gradually extended and now reaches the 5 miles to Slaggyford. The eventual aim of the railway is to reach Haltwhistle, where space has been reserved alongside the existing permanent way. A Class 156 DMU arrives at Haltwhistle, where the STR eventually hopes to make its northern terminus. In the right of the background is Alston Arches.

The line has some notable architectural features. Both Alston and Slaggyford stations are listed Grade II, as is Alston Arches viaduct, while Lambley viaduct is listed Grade II*. It is thought that the architect of the viaducts was Sir George Barclay Bruce. A multiple unit passes over Lambley Viaduct in September 1973. (Photo: John Ragla)

The Maryport & Carlisle Railway

The M&C received its Act on 12 July 1837. The engineer was George Stephenson. Work started at both ends of the line. Maryport to Arkleby Pit, near Aspatria, opened on 15 July 1840 and to Aspatria itself on 12 April 1841. Carlisle to Wigton opened on 3 May 1843, and Wigton to Aspatria on 10 February 1845. Maryport station is seen in 1951. It only ever had one platform. The station was also the headquarters of the company. These buildings were demolished in the 1970s. (Photo: Walter Dendy)

On 21 April 1995 a Class 153 DMU heads into the station with a service for Carlisle. The station buildings have gone but the layout remains much the same, with the Down and Up main lines either side of the signal box and a loop for trains calling at the single platform.

A 1961 view of Bullgill station looking south towards Bullgill Junction. This was the junction for the 6.5-mile Derwent Branch, opened on 1 June 1861. This line joined the LNW Cockermouth line at Brigham Junction and the M&C had running powers through to Cockermouth, although this involved reversals at Bullgill and Brigham. There were stations at Dearham, Linefoot, and Papcastle. There was also a private station at Dovenby for the use of the inhabitants of Dovenby Hall. This line lost its passenger service in 1935 and Bullgill station closed on 7 March 1960. (Photo: Ben Brooksbank)

On 21 April 1995 Class 142 'Pacer' No. 142037 approaches Aspatria station with a service from Carlisle. The signal box seen in the background, dating from 1891, was the last surviving example of a Maryport & Carlisle Railway design box. Sadly it was abolished in 1998 and subsequently demolished.

Brayton was originally a private station for the use of Sir Wilfred Lawson, a director of the M&C. From 1848 it became available to the public. It closed in 1950.

The magnificent neoclassical station at Wigton *c.* 1890. Today only three intermediate stations survive on the M&C. Other stations that have closed are Cummerdale, Curthwaite, Leegate, and Dearham Bridge. After an initial troubled phase the M&C went on to become an extremely prosperous railway.

In 1895 the M&C provided a passenger service of seven trains daily between Maryport and Carlisle. Journey time was between one hour and one hour ten minutes. One hundred years later, in April 1995 a Class 142 'Pacer' approaches Wigton station with a service for Carlisle. Notice the water column, which looks complete and serviceable.

Dalston station is the last station before Carlisle. The layout today remains as in this 1995 view. The oil depot remains active. The first terminus of the M&C in Carlisle was at Crown Street. It then shared the Newcastle & Carlisle's station at London Road before finally transferring to Citadel station in 1851.

In 1861 the Carlisle & Silloth Bay Railway expressed an intention to open up the coalfield around Mealsgate by building a branch from their Abbey station. Nothing came of this but it spurred the M&C into building a branch themselves. The Bolton loop was opened from Aspatria to Aikbank Junction in 1866. The eastern end of the line was abandoned for a while but reinstated at the end of the 1870s. There were stations at Baggrow, Mealsgate and High Blaithwaite. This is Mealsgate. On the right is the single through line and on the left a connection to a long siding which followed the path of an old wagonway.

Minimal facilities at High Blaithwaite. The small building is the signal box. The two collieries on the loop were All Hallows between Mealsgate and Baggrow, and Brayton Domain to the west of Baggrow. Passenger traffic was never very important and the line east of High Blaithwaite closed in 1921. Passenger services were withdrawn from the rest of the loop in 1930. The remaining stretch of line between Mealsgate and Aspatria closed completely in 1952.

The M&C built many of its own locomotives. At the Grouping twenty-one of the thirty-three locomotives absorbed into the LMS had been built in the company's workshops. This Class 13 2-4-0 No. 13, dating from 1873, was designed by Hugh Smellie, the Locomotive Superintendent between 1870 and 1878. It was withdrawn in 1925.

The company also ordered from outside contractors. This 0-4-0T No. R3 was the Maryport Docks shunter. It was built by Neilson, Reid & Company in 1880. It had previously carried the number 15.

Carlisle

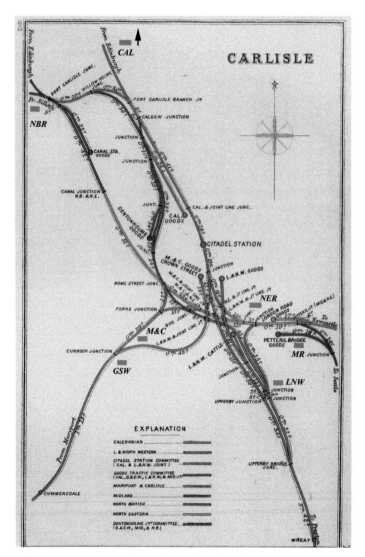

This Railway Clearing House map, dating from shortly before the First World War, shows the extraordinary situation at Carlisle, where no less than seven different railway companies were represented. Although by this time all seven companies used Citadel station for their passenger trains, for goods services each had their own depot. On top of this were the locomotive depots, shown on the map by red rectangles, carriage sheds, wagon repair workshops, and other ancillary buildings. A veritable railway town.

Carlisle first appeared on the railway map with the arrival of the Newcastle & Carlisle Railway in 1836. The station of the N&C was at London Road. When the Lancaster & Carlisle Railway reached Carlisle in 1846 it used London Road station as a temporary measure before the opening of Carlisle Citadel station. The Maryport & Carlisle Railway also ran some trains to London Road until 1851, after which its trains ran to Citadel. The Newcastle & Carlisle was amalgamated with the North Eastern Railway in 1862 and passenger services to London Road ceased. In 1881 the station was demolished and a goods station built in its place. These are the buildings seen here in a photograph dating from 1991.

In the 1990s the smaller building was demolished and the rails lifted. The railway land is now scheduled for redevelopment but the goods depot remains as it is a listed building. Its importance is due to the fact that it is an intact urban goods station. The architect was William Bell.

Carlisle Citadel station was constructed in the years 1847/48 in a Tudor style to the design of Sir William Tite. It was later enlarged. The exterior is seen in a view dating from 1925. The building is listed Grade II*.

In late Victorian times a pair of Midland Railway Johnson 2-4-0s stand at Carlisle Citadel platform 2 waiting to depart with a train for the south.

At the other end of the station staff pose with a Maryport & Carlisle locomotive. No. 8 was a Smellie-designed Class 13 2-4-0, introduced in 1876.

In 1947 Rebuilt Royal Scot No. 6108 *Seaforth Highlander* departs from Carlisle station with an express for Scotland. No. 6103 was built in 1927, rebuilt in 1943 and withdrawn in 1963. (Photo: courtesy of Science Museum)

In 1959 Class 40 No. D211 is a sign of the new order as it stands on the Down goods line at Carlisle waiting to take over its train. At the platform is Stanier 'Jubilee' 4-6-0 No. 45657 *Tyrwhitt*. A number of the Jubilee class were named after famous admirals. Sir Reginald Tyrwhitt was an admiral at the time of the First World War. (Photo: Alan Murray-Rust)

The Glasgow to Euston 'Caledonian' had just one stop between Glasgow and Euston, at Carlisle. The Up service is seen passing over the canal goods lines as it leaves Carlisle on 12 August 1960 headed by Stanier 'Pacific' 4-6-2 No. 46250 *City of Lichfield*. Behind the second carriage of the train is the bridge that carries the Maryport & Carlisle lines as they diverge away from the main line. (Photo: Ben Brooksbank)

Part of the complex of lines to the south of Carlisle station. The lines from right to left are North Eastern shunt neck; Down and Up Newcastle; Newcastle goods Up; Newcastle goods Down; and the two lines on the extreme left are the Up and Down through goods lines. The bridge carries the West Coast Main Line, and behind, unseen, is the bridge carrying the Down and Up Maryport & Carlisle lines. The Class 156 unit is heading for Morpeth.

On 15 September 2020 'Royal Scot' Class 4-6-0 No. 46115 *Scots Guardsman* stands at the north end of Carlisle station, having just arrived with 'The Dalesman' special train from York via the Settle & Carlisle line.

Also at the north end on 15 September is Scotrail unit No. 156510 waiting to depart with a service to Dumfries.

On the same date at the south end the 14.52 Avanti West Coast Edinburgh to London Euston Pendolino stands at the platform waiting to depart.

On 21 April 1995, having just passed Petteril Bridge Junction, Class 60 No. 60056 *Kinder Low* heads east on the Carlisle to Newcastle line with a train of tanks. In the background is the Carlisle London Road Coal Concentration Depot, since demolished.

Upperby depot was closed in 1968 and demolished in 1979. The carriage sheds, seen here, were retained for servicing and maintenance. They are seen shortly before closure in 1995. The locomotive on the left is Gresley Pacific 4-6-2 No. 60007 *Sir Nigel Gresley*. The sheds were demolished in 2016.

Currock is the former Glasgow & South Western loco shed. It was opened in 1896 and converted to a wagon repair depot in 1924, a purpose which it continued to serve until closure in 2007. It is seen here in 1995. It is the only surviving steam era shed in Carlisle.

Carlisle Kingmoor shed is seen on 29 April 1967. Among those on shed are several 9F 2-10-0s, a 'Black Five' 4-6-0, a 'Jinty' 0-6-0 and a Class 08 shunter. (Photo: J. W. Sutherland)

The Furness Railway

Even before the time of the railway Barrow was exporting iron ore from the mines around Dalton and Lindal. In the 1840s this amounted to some 40,000 tons per annum. The Earl of Burlington asked James Walker to investigate the feasibility of a railway line to Barrow from the mines at Dalton and the slate quarries at Kirkby. The result was the Furness Railway, the Act for which was received on 23 May 1844. The planned lines were from Lindal via Roose to Barrow, with branches to Kirkby and Rampside. The purpose of the latter was to connect to Piel station on Roa Island, from where there was to be a steamer service to Fleetwood. The FR purchased the Roa Island enterprise in 1853. A late nineteenth-century view of Piel station. The locomotive is a Class E1 2-4-0 built by Sharp Stewart in 1873.

The main line opened on 3 June 1846 but only as far as Croslands, half a mile east of Dalton. An Act of 3 June 1846 authorised the extension from Croslands to Ulverston. The line reached Lindal by 6 May 1851. Meanwhile in February 1848 a 3.5-mile extension to Broughton was completed, the main purpose of which was to handle copper from the Coniston mines. Furness Abbey station opened in 1847, and until 1873 through trains reversed here. The station closed on 25 September 1950.

An Up train arrives at Lindal station. The station opened on 6 May 1851 and closed just over a century later.

The famous Lindal hole, which opened up beneath a locomotive on 22 September 1892. The crew were able to jump clear but the locomotive was lost.

The creation of the Ulverston & Lancaster Railway in 1851 spurred the FR directors to complete the line to Ulverston, which was reached on 7 June 1854. Roose Junction to Barrow was doubled in 1854, Croslands to Lindal in 1857, and Lindal to Ulverston in 1858. In the same year the Dalton Junction to Goldmire Junction curve was opened, thus allowing trains to bypass Barrow. A new curve was constructed at Foxfield to connect the Whitehaven & Furness Junction Railway and FR. The station at Broughton was closed and a new through Broughton station opened in readiness for the Coniston Railway. A new station was built at Foxfield. The present station, designed by Paley and Austin, dates to 1879. On 4 August 1951 a Stanier 5MT 4-6-0 stands at the head of the 06.40 Euston to Workington train. (Photo: Walter Dendy)

A view taken from the other direction on the same date. (Photo: Walter Dendy)

Foxfield station on 26 October 1989. The platform overall roof and goods shed have gone but the Paley and Austin designed signal box and shelter remain.

The year 1859 saw the first two blast furnaces at Barrow come into production, using ore mined near Park. On 26 May 1862 the U&LR became part of the FR, followed in 1866 by the W&FJR. On 29 April 1863 the new Strand station opened and the old Barrow station became an engine shed. In 1867 the Midland Railway steamers to the Isle of Man and to Belfast started to use the Piel harbour. From 1881 the ships used the Ramsden Dock until 1904 when the crossings were switched to Heysham. The Piel line closed in 1936. At Ramsden Dock station stands a Pettigrew K2 'Larger Seagull' 4-4-0, a design dating from the end of the nineteenth century.

In 1882 the new line from Salthouse Junction to Park Junction opened together with the new station at Barrow Central. The Strand station became the railway institute. Barrow Central was destroyed in an air raid in 1941. The new station opened eighteen years later. Barrow Central station in the early years of the twentieth century with yet another 'Larger' Seagull 4-4-0.

In September 1976 a Class 108 DMU stands at platform 2 at Barrow-in-Furness station. (Photo: Geoffrey Skelsey)

Five years later on 30 October 1981 in miserable wet weather Class 47 No. 47434 heads out of the station with a train of steel bar.

On 21 July 1845 the W&FJR received its authorising Act. It was completed from Whitehaven to Ravenglass by 21 July 1849, to Bootle by 8 July 1850 and throughout by 1 November 1850. The W&FJ met the FR Broughton extension line about a mile south of Broughton station. The northern terminus was at Preston Street (previously Newtown). It was later used as a goods shed, as seen here, still in use in 1990. It has since been demolished.

Intermediate stations on the W&FJR were at St Bees, Nethertown, Braystones, Sellafield, Seascale, Drigg, Ravenglass, Eskmeals, Bootle, Silecroft, Holborn Hill, Underhill (closed in 1860), and Green Road (opened in 1853). There was no connection between the Whitehaven Junction Railway and the W&FJR until the 1,333-yard Bransty tunnel was completed in July 1852. Passenger trains from the south continued to terminate at Preston Street until 1855 when alterations at the WJR terminus allowed trains from the south to use that station, though even so this meant that trains had to back in. This situation continued until 1874 when new through platforms were constructed at Bransty, which then became a LNW/FR joint station. Corkickle station opened in 1855 as a replacement for Preston Street, which became a goods depot. These two photos taken on 2 June 1990 perhaps illustrate as well as any the dramatic changes that have taken place in the last thirty or forty years as regards freight traffic. The first photograph is taken from near Corkickle No. 1 box, looking towards Corkickle No. 2.

The second photograph is taken from near No. 2 box, looking in the opposite direction. Everything in these photographs has now disappeared – track, sidings, gantry, signals, and both signal boxes. All that remains is a single track plain line. The train approaching Corkickle station is the 10.23 Barrow to Carlisle.

On 8 July 1997 at St Bees the driver of a nuclear flask train hauled by Class 37 No. 37262 surrenders the token for the single line section from Ravenglass and collects the key token for the next section to Whitehaven.

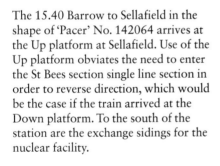

The 15.40 Barrow to Sellafield in the shape of 'Pacer' No. 142064 arrives at the Up platform at Sellafield. Use of the Up platform obviates the need to enter the St Bees section single line section in order to reverse direction, which would be the case if the train arrived at the Down platform. To the south of the station are the exchange sidings for the nuclear facility.

In July 1997 DMU No. 153358 arrives at Drigg with the 13.50 Lancaster to Carlisle. The signal box is an FR type 1 dating to *c*. 1871. At the north of Drigg station is the connection to the sidings of the Low Level Waste Repository.

At Bootle 'Pacer' No. 142027 arrives with the 13.03 Carlisle to Lancaster. The signal box is another FR type 1. The box here and at Drigg are the only two survivors of this type. It is listed Grade II.

To see the quiet country station of Millom today it might be difficult to believe that it was once the focal point of a vast industrial complex. In 1856 prospectors discovered a major deposit of haematite iron ore. This deposit at Hodbarrow to the south of Millom turned out to be the largest in the whole world at that time. The majority of the ore was moved by sea despite a branch to Hodbarrow being opened by the FR in 1867. The growth of production was exponential, reaching half a million tons a year in the period 1905 to 1909. Millom Ironworks, which was located between the mine and Millom station and served by the same railway line, started production in 1867. In 1909 the FR carried away 43,000 tons of pig iron and brought in more than a quarter of a million tons of coal and coke. Another railway line connected the Redhills limestone quarry to the ironworks. The Hodbarrow branch passed through the centre of the ironworks.

On 2 September 1967 Barclay 0-4-0T
Prince John is seen at Millom with
a pair of slag hoppers. (Photo: J. W.
Sutherland)

This was the date of a visiting railtour
and *Prince John* is seen together with
Stanier 5MT 4-6-0 No. 45134.
(Photo: J. W. Sutherland)

Altogether in the Hodbarrow peninsular
there were some 40 miles of railways.
Nearly fifty different locomotives saw
service at the ironworks. Two have been
preserved. Barclay 0-4-0T No. 2333
was initially located at Steamtown
Carnforth but from 1978 has been at
the Lakeside & Haverthwaite Railway.
Barclay 0-4-0T No. 929 *Alexandra*
went in the reverse direction, originally
being at the L&H and presently being
located at Criggion in Wales. *Alexandra*
is seen at Steamtown, Carnforth, where
it resided for a short period. (Photo:
Hugh Llewelyn)

Both the mine and the ironworks went into rapid decline in the depression following the First World War and both revived in the late thirties and during the war as Britain rearmed. After the second conflict both the mine and the ironworks were nationalised and then privatised. Competition from other sources of ore and of iron sent both the mine and works into decline in the 1960s and production at both ceased in 1968. The original name of the settlement, which later became Millom, was Holborn Hill. The new name came about following the construction of a new town built in the 1860s to ease a severe shortage of accommodation. Thus it was that the town was named after the ironworks. The railway followed suit, renaming the station in June 1866. On 30 October 1981 a Class 108 DMU waits to depart from Millom with the 15.00 service to Lancaster.

On 8 July 1997 pair of DRS Class 20s approach Green Road station bearing the headboard 'Milkliner 2000'.

Ireleth Gate station opened in April 1851 and closed in October 1857. A newly built station designed by Paley and Austin opened on 1 April 1868. It was renamed Askam on 1 January 1875. Both the station buildings and signal box are Grade II listed. The box is an FR type 2 dating from 1890.

The Ulverstone & Lancaster Railway

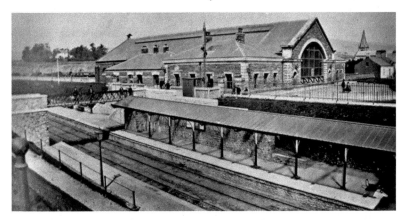

A number of schemes had been put forward to link Ulverston with the national network and in fact three such schemes had been put before Parliament in 1845, though nothing came of any of them. In 1858 the John Brogdens, father and son, commissioned a survey for a line between Ulverston and the Lancaster & Carlisle Railway. A bill was put before Parliament in 1851 and received royal assent on 24 July the same year. In the following November the first sod was cut but it would be another six years before the 20-mile line between Ulverston and Carnforth would be complete. The railway opened to goods traffic on 10 August 1857 and to passengers later in the same month. The line was doubled between Ulverston and the Leven Viaduct in 1860 and between the Leven Viaduct and Cark in 1861. The U&LR was purchase by the FR in January 1862 and it was that company which doubled the line between Carnforth and Cark in 1863. The first U&LR station at Ulverston opened in 1857. In the background is the FR station of 1854, which was subsequently used as a goods station.

Between 1876 and 1878 Ulverston station was rebuilt in an Italianate style to the design of Paley and Austin. The line with a platform either side was built to allow easy transfer to Lakeside trains. The station is listed Grade II.

The main difficulty encountered in building the line was of course the building of the viaducts across the Leven and the Kent. The viaducts consisted of cast-iron columns driven into the sand surmounted by wrought-iron girders supporting the trackbed. Doubling of the track across the viaducts entailed adding an extra column on the inland side. This took place in 1863. In 1885/6 the girders and decking were replaced. By the early years of the twentieth century the viaducts were in a poor condition but work to strengthen them did not start until 1913. This work consisted of encasing the columns in an envelope of brick and concrete on a masonry base. The Leven Viaduct was dealt with first, followed by the Kent Viaduct, all work being completed by 1917. It is this work that gives the viaducts their characteristic appearance today. Further work was carried out in the 1990s and again in 2006 when remedial work included the laying of a concrete trackbed. The Leven Viaduct is seen *c.* 1890.

The Leven Viaduct had been built with an opening span to allow shipping to reach the port of Greenodd. This was a considerable nuisance to the railway and an agreement was reached with the owner of Greenodd wharf to the effect that the railway would build a branch to Greenodd and another to the Ulverston Canal in exchange for which the railway could remove the opening section. Both lines opened in 1869. The FR decided to build a new line from Plumpton Junction to Barrow via the coast, the main purpose of which was to avoid trains having to be banked from Barrow up to Lindal. Always known as the Bardsea branch the line did not even get as far as the eponymous village, reaching only as far as the Priory station, built to serve the Conishead Priory hydropathic station. The line was finally opened for passenger traffic in 1883. The only passengers were those heading for the priory and a service of two return trains daily soon became just one. The intermediate station of North Lonsdale Crossing was opened in 1888.

The new line served a quarry and a number of industrial sites, foremost of which was the North Lonsdale Ironworks. Most of these industries had closed by the outbreak of the Second World War. In 1948 Glaxo built a factory in the site of the ironworks, which was served by rail. By 1967 the only traffic on the branch was fuel oil. This continued until April 1994 after which the only use for the line came on 22 May 1995 when the royal train was stabled there overnight. In 2000 the line was severed at Plumpton Junction, Plumpton box demolished and the branch and sidings lifted. A Class 156 unit passes Plumpton Junction with an eastbound service on 8 July 1997. Notice the signals for the branch, still standing, although the branch was out of use at this time.

The Lakeside Branch. As we have seen the FR was obliged to build a branch as far as Greenodd in return for being able to close the opening section of the Leven Viaduct. It was decided to extend this line to Newby Bridge in order to connect with the Windermere steamer service. The Act, which was passed on 16 July 1866, authorised a 7-mile branch from Plumpton Junction to Newby Bridge as well as a curve from the east, thus making a triangular junction. The line opened to Greenodd on 18 March 1869 and to Newby Bridge on 23 April. A further half-mile extension to Windermere Lakeside was opened on 1 June. A station at Haverthwaite was opened on 1 September. In 1872 the FR purchased the Windermere United Steam Yacht Co. Ltd. This is the steamer *Swift*.

In 1905 Newby Bridge Motor Car Platform opened, at which time a steam railmotor was introduced on the branch. The line slowly declined after the Second World War and from 1938 both steamer and rail passenger services became seasonal only. During that conflict services were withdrawn and only restored on 30 June 1946. In the peak summer period of 1953 there were six or seven services on weekdays between Ulverston and Lakeside with through trains to Blackpool and Morecambe. On Sundays there were four services including through carriages to Morecambe. Trains did not stop at Greenodd or Haverthwaite where passenger trains had ceased to call from 30 September 1946 but were not officially withdrawn until 13 June 1955. The line was listed for closure in the Beeching Report and the last train ran on 5 September 1965. Freight traffic continued until April 1967. An attempt was made by enthusiasts to buy the whole line. This failed but in 1970 a group completed the purchase of the 3.5 miles between Lakeside and Haverthwaite. In 1973 the Lakeside and Haverthwaite railway ran its first public trains. On 4 August 1951 Fowler 4MT 2-6-4T No. 42376 stands at Lakeside with a train for Ulverston. (Photo: Walter Dendy)

The station buildings at Cark. These are the original buildings dating from the opening of the railway. The station was originally Cark-in-Cartmell. It became Cark and Cartmel in 1906. It was the station for Holker Hall, the home of Lord Cavendish, one of the main movers behind both the FR and the U&L.

On 6 June 1992 Stanier 8F 2-8-0 No. 48151 passes the site of Wraysholme Halt with a Carnforth to Barrow special steam shuttle train. The halt was opened in 1911. It was never in the public timetable and went out of use *c.* 1922. There was a branch to a site where Vickers were proposing to build an airship factory. The factory was never built.

Heading in the opposite direction with a Barrow to Carnforth service on 31 August 1958 are Stanier 'Black Five' 4-6-0 No. 45199 and Fowler 4MT 2-6-4T No. 42395. The woman in the photograph appears to be carrying a large ham! (Photo: J. W. Sutherland)

Grange station in the 1880s. The station was rebuilt by Paley and Austin in 1864 and is listed Grade II.

In June 1992 Class 60 No. 60066 *John Logie Baird* is seen approaching Grange station with the returning empties from Padiham Power Station.

The Kent Viaduct with Stanier 8F No. 48151 on a Barrow to Carnforth shuttle.

Heading in the opposite direction is a Class 31 with a nuclear flask train bound for Sellafield. The importance of this traffic for the railway has been instrumental in keeping this line open – once proposed for closure.

As Class 150 No. 150150 draws away from Arnside station with the 10.48 Manchester Victoria to Barrow it has been brought to a halt by the signalman to be warned of problems ahead on the line.

On 6 June 1992 a Class 156 unit passes Arnside signal box with the 11.35 Barrow to Lancaster. The box is an FR type 4 dating from 1897 and is a listed structure. Arnside was the junction for the Hincaster branch.

The Hincaster branch. In 1846 the Furness & Yorkshire Union Railway proposed a line from Arnside to Kirkby Lonsdale. This was opposed by the LNW but a modified scheme for a line from Arnside to Hincaster Junction, 3.75 miles south of Oxenholme, proposed by the FR was approved in 1867. It was to be another nine years before the 5.25-mile single-track line was opened. There were intermediate stations at Sandside and Heversham. This new route avoided the reversal at Carnforth of trains from the north-east. There were also a number of through passenger trains utilising the route. Local trains ran between Grange over Sands and Kendal. This was the famous 'Kendal Tommy'. The trains were worked by Sharp Stewart 2-2-2 well tanks until the 1890s. At Grange-over-Sands Sharp Stewart 2-2-2WT No. 37 waits to depart for Kendal.

In 1895 there were four return trains with an additional service on Mondays. The passenger service ceased in 1942 but coke trains for Barrow continued until 1963. After that, only the section between Arnside and Sandside remained open until 1971 to service the quarry at the latter location, after which the line was closed completely. Heversham station is seen here.

Kents Bank station, another Paley and Austin design, dating from 1865.

The Furness and Midland Joint Line

By 1866 the FR found itself hemmed in by the LNW at both ends of its network by virtue of the acquisition of the WJR by the LNW at one end and its lease of the Lancaster & Carlisle at the other. The Midland was keen to find a new port for its steamers to Belfast and the Isle of Man due to problems at Morecambe and thus it was agreed that the two companies would build a joint line from Wennington to Carnforth. This would give the MR access to Barrow for its ships and the FR access for its ore traffic to the West Riding. The line was opened to freight on 10 April 1867 and to passengers on 6 June of the same year. There were stations at Carnforth F&M Junction, Melling, Arkholme, and Borwick. The last three stations were closed by 1960 but the line still sees passenger services. Arkholme station seen in 1990, thirty years after closure.

On 31 May 1990 a 'Pacer' departs from Wennington with the 12.33 Leeds to Morecambe. Wennington signal box was closed in 2006, having been switched out for many years, and donated to the Poulton & Wyre Railway.

In 1880 a new connecting line was built to give the MR access to Carnforth. At the same time the FR station at F&M Junction was closed. It was located near these signals controlled by Carnforth F&M Junction signal box. The left-hand signals are for Carnforth East Junction and the line to Wennington, the right-hand pair are for Carnforth station. The spare doll was for the line, now removed, which avoided Carnforth station and connected directly to the WCML.

A closer view of F&M Junction. The lines to the right lead to Carnforth station, those on the left to Carnforth East box, seen in the distance.

Carnforth East box. The signal on the left is the Up home from Carnforth F&M Junction, and on the right the Up home from Carnforth Station Junction. In the centre carrying the Down signals is a Midland Railway wooden balanced bracket.

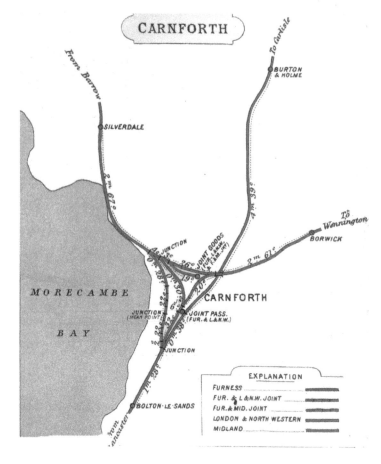

The layout here has now been completely changed. Both signal boxes have been abolished and there is no longer a through route to the Wennington line. What was once a triangular junction is now configured as a Y. This Clearing House map shows the layout as it was before the First World War.

Carnforth

The redundant signal box at the north end of Carnforth station dates from FR days, *c.* 1882. It has been out of use since 1903. It bears the motto of the Cavendish family *'cavendo tutus'*.

The main line platforms at Carnforth in 1907. These platforms were taken out of use in 1970 and main line trains can no longer stop here.

Before that date, on 7 June 1968 Stanier 5MT No. 44894 stands on the Up Main with a service from Windermere, substituting for a failed DMU. (Photo: J. W. Sutherland)

On 25 August 1964 Fowler 4F 0-6-0 No. 44386 heads a Class E freight train south through Carnforth. These engines, the basic design of which dated back to 1873, were produced in huge numbers over a long period: 762 examples were built between 1911 and 1941. (Photo: Ben Brooksbank)

Just two platforms are now in use at Carnforth. On 27 November 1982 Maunsell 'Lord Nelson' Class 4-6-0 No. 850 *Lord Nelson* sets off from platform two with the Cumbrian Mountain Pullman.

Furness Railway locomotives

The FR had a large variety of locomotives, nearly all built by outside manufacturers. The classification system used here is that devised by Bob Rush: Class A2. Two locomotives were purchased from Bury, Curtis & Kennedy in 1846, Nos 3 and 4. They had cylinders 13 in x 24 in and 4 ft 9 in wheels. No. 4, seen here, was withdrawn in 1898, while No. 3 continued in service until 1900 and was then preserved.

F.R. OLD TANK ENGINE. (1866-1896).

Class B3. No. 35, a 2-2-2 well tank, was built by Sharp, Stewart & Co. in 1866, one of six of the same type, with 5 ft 6 in driving wheels and cylinders 15 in x 18 in. No. 35 was withdrawn as No. 35A in 1898 and the sold to the Weston, Clevedon & Portishead Railway.

Class J1. These 2-4-2Ts were rebuilds of class E1 2-4-0 tender engines, introduced in 1870. A total of seven were rebuilt in 1891. These engines spent much of their time on the Lakeside branch.

F.R. TANK ENGINE.

Class L3. A development of earlier L1 and L2 classes, these engines were built by North British in 1907. They had 5ft 1in drivers and cylinders 18" x 26". No.110 was withdrawn as LMS No. 11639 in 1931.

Class N1. These 4-6-4T 'Baltics', known as 'Jumbos' were the last express passenger design for the FR. This class of five locomotives was built by Kitson & Co. and delivered in 1920/21. They mainly worked mail and express trains between Carnforth and Whitehaven. Driving wheels were 5 ft 8 in and cylinders 19.5 in x 26 in. Boiler pressure was 170psi. They were the only British Baltics with inside cylinders. No. 115 was withdrawn in 1935.

Class K1. Towards the end of the nineteenth century the FR needed a more powerful express passenger locomotive for the Irish boat trains. The answer was this 4-4-0 was supplied by Sharp, Stewart & Co. in 1891. These engines had 5 ft 6 in drivers and cylinders 17 in x 24 in. Popularly known as 'Seagulls' they remained in service until the mid-1920s. No. 123 was the first to go, being withdrawn in 1925.

F.R. PASSENGER ENGINE.

Class K3. The design of this class of 4-4-0s was in the hands of the Chief Mechanical Engineer of the FR, William Pettigrew, and they were built by Sharp, Stewart & Co. in 1901. Cylinders were 26 in x 18 in and driving wheels 6 ft 6 in. Just four in the class, two were stationed at Whitehaven and two at Carnforth whence they handled all express passenger services for over twelve years. No. 129 was withdrawn as LMS No. 10146 in 1930.

Class D5. Another design by Pettigrew was this 0-6-0 of 1913. Altogether thirty-five engines of this type were built between 1913 and 1920, thirty-one by North British and four by Kitson. No. 52509 entered service in 1920 and survived until 1956. It is seen at Workington loco shed in 1951. (Photo: Walter Dendy)

The Lancaster & Carlisle Railway

After much discussion about possible routes from Lancaster to Carlisle, including one via the Cumbrian coast, the Lancaster and Carlisle Railway Act was passed on 6 June 1844. All the railway companies represented in the parts of the west coast route already built would be investors in the new company. The Engineer in Chief was Joseph Locke. Work started just six weeks after the Act was passed and a single line was completed between Lancaster and Kendal by 22 September 1846. By January 1847 the double track line was completed throughout. Meanwhile the Caledonian Railway was under construction and was completed between Glasgow and Carlisle in February 1848. The line was worked by the LNW until 1857, then briefly by the L&C, before reverting once more to the LNW in 1859. All of the stations on the L&C in Cumbria, apart from Penrith, Oxenholme and Carlisle, are closed. Burton on Holme closed in 1950. It is seen here in October 1961. (Photo: Ben Brooksbank)

Oxenholme was so named from the early 1860s. Before that it was known as Kendal Junction. Indeed its main purpose was to provide a junction station for Kendal, it having proved too difficult to build the main line through Kendal itself. Today it is Oxenholme the Lake District. This view dates from the Edwardian period. The platform on the left was for the Kendal/ Windermere branch.

A view taken from further south shows the engine shed, opened in 1880 and closed in 1962. On the left is the water tower and coaling stage. There was an allocation of eight or nine locomotives to work the branch, in the latter years mainly Stanier 2-6-4Ts. In the distance Oxenholme No. 2 signal box can be seen.

The Windermere Branch. The Kendal & Windermere Railway was incorporated on 30 June 1845 and opened throughout on 4 January 1847. This 10.25-mile line had intermediate stations at Kendal, Burneside, and Staveley. Getting into financial difficulties the line was leased by the L&C from 1 May 1858. In the 1930s Whale 2P 4-4-2T No. 6811 sets off from Oxenholme with a service for Windermere.

Many years later, on 31 May 1990, on the now singled line, a Class 143 'Pacer' nears Oxenholme with a service from Windermere. The branch is now worked by Class 195 units.

Between Oxenholme and Tebay were the stations of Grayrigg and Low Gill. The latter station was rebuilt in a new location to accommodate the opening of the line from Ingleton in 1861. It closed in 1960, while Grayrigg closed in 1954. Tebay was not one of the original stations on the L&C. It opened in 1851 and was rebuilt in 1861 to form a junction with the South Durham and Lancaster Union line from Barnard Castle. Tebay shed opened in 1861, its main purpose being to provide banking engines for trains ascending Shap. Having no further purpose, it closed along with the station at the end of steam in 1968. Pulling into the station on 7 October 1961 is Royal Scot 7P 4-6-0 No.46127 *The Old Comtemptibles* at the head of the 09.05 Crewe to Perth. (Photo: Ben Brooksbank)

Having got the road, an unidentified Stanier 8F 2-8-0 pulls away from Tebay with a freight train. The loco shed is behind the wall on the right. (Photo: David Spencer)

Dillicar water troughs were located between Low Gill and Tebay, a chance for locomotives to be replenished before or after the climb to Shap. Princess Royal Class 8P 4-6-2 No. 6206 *Princess Marie Louise* is seen with a southbound express in LMS days. Curious that the engine is paired with a Fowler tender. (Photo: courtesy of Science Museum)

Apart from a 5-mile respite between Grayrigg and Tebay , the West Coast line climbs continuously for 30 miles between Carnforth and Shap Summit, the last 4 miles being at 1 in 75. Slogging up the grade in 1945 is Stanier 8F No. 8460 with a long train of mineral wagons. (Photo: courtesy of Science Museum)

Also in LMS days, climbing Shap without assistance is unrebuilt Royal Scot 6P 4-6-0 No. 6109 *Royal Engineer*. In its rebuilt form as No. 46109, this engine was withdrawn at the end of 1962.

Clifton became a junction station with the opening in 1862 of the Eden Valley Railway, which connected via a south facing spur. The opening of the Cockermouth, Keswick & Penrith Railway in 1863 created a viable route from the north-east to West Cumbria, except for the south facing spur at Clifton. Accordingly a new northern spur was created and a new line built from Eamont Bridge Junction on the WCML passing under the CK&P and joining it at Redhills Junction, thus avoiding the necessity for freight trains to reverse at Penrith. Clifton was renamed Clifton and Lowther in 1877. The southern spur was removed in 1977. This is a view of the station from the south.

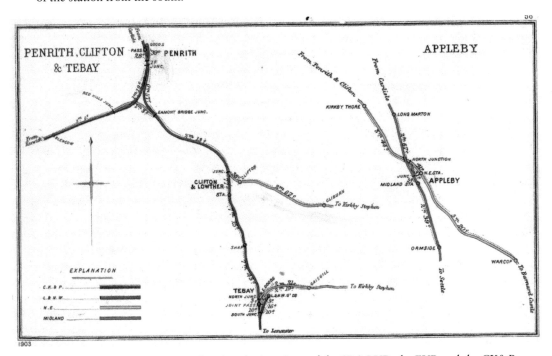

The 1914 Clearing House map showing the junctions of the SD&LUR, the EVR and the CK&P with the L&C.

Penrith station like the others on the L&C was designed by Sir William Tite. It is Grade II listed. In the 1920s the charabancs, probably provided by the LMS, are ready for a tour of the Lakes. (Photo: courtesy of Science Museum)

A 1925 view of the station looking south. Notice the large amount of luggage distributed along the platform waiting for the next Down service. (Photo: courtesy of Science Museum)

On 11 August 1951 Royal Scot 7P 4-6-0 No. 46105 *Cameron Highlander* and 2P 4-4-0 No. 40631 pull away from Penrith with the 10.45 Glasgow to Manchester Victoria. Note that No. 46105 has yet to be fitted with smoke deflectors. (Photo: Ben Brooksbank)

The North Western

The North Western Railway was incorporated on 26 July 1846 with powers to build a line from Skipton to Low Gill, on the L&C, plus a branch from Clapham to Lancaster. Once the LNWR was formed the NWR inevitably became known as the Little North Western. By 30 July 1849 the 30 miles from Skipton to Ingleton were completed and a service of four trains daily was put in place. However, once the NWR route to Lancaster was completed the passenger service on the 4-mile branch to Ingleton was withdrawn. The NWR no longer had the resources to complete the line to Low Gill and it was the L&C that completed the line, which opened in 1861. The L&C, now leased by the LNW, had its own station at Ingleton. It was the LNW's obstructive attitude towards the MR, now the lessees of the NWR, which caused the MR to plan its own route to Carlisle and Scotland. Once the Settle & Carlisle line was open the Ingleton line settled back to being a country backwater, instead of the through route to Scotland for which it had been intended. Barbon station is seen in September 1962. The station had long been closed but freight traffic continued to pass through. (Photo: Ben Brooksbank)

There were stations at Ingleton, Kirkby Lonsdale, Barbon, Middleton and Sedbergh. The LNW station at Ingleton closed in 1917. In 1895 in the Down direction there were three services between Ingleton (MR) and Tebay and one to Low Gill only. All these Down trains had a long wait at Ingleton (LNW), presumably to carry out shunting. In the Up direction there were three services: Tebay to Ingleton (MR) and one to Ingleton (MR). In 1953, the last year of passenger operation, there were six trains in each direction with an additional service on Saturdays. Passenger services ceased on the 30 January 1954 and the line closed completely in 1965. Kirkby Lonsdale station photographed in October 1989.

The Midland Railway

Thwarted in its attempts to reach a satisfactory agreement with the LNW for the use of the Lancaster & Carlisle Railway to reach Scotland, the Midland Railway finally decided to build its own independent route to Carlisle. It successfully put forward a bill to Parliament and received its Act on 16 July 1866. In the meantime the LNW had become more amenable and a deal was struck in 1868 giving the MR use of the L&C. The MR now wished to abandon its plans for an independent route but the Lancashire and Yorkshire & North British railways, which had previously supported the bill, insisted that the line be built. Parliament took their view of the matter and so it came about that the MR had to build a line they no longer wanted or needed. Blea Moor marked the end of the 'Long Drag', the 15-mile 1 in 100 climb from Settle Junction. In 1988 Class 47 No. 47555 *The Commonwealth Spirit* has completed the climb and will shortly enter Blea Moor tunnel.

Some time later a hybrid Class 108/Class 101 unit passes with a local service to Carlisle. Not long after this photograph was taken the Down goods loop and Down refuge siding, seen in the distance, were removed. Notice the pilot engine by the signal box.

Travelling in the opposite direction on the same day is No. 47610 with a diverted WCML service. There can be few more lonely outposts on the railway than the signal box at Blea Moor. It is an LMS type 11c and dates from 1941.

Construction of the line was a heroic task given the nature of the countryside through which it had to pass. Along the 78 miles between Settle Junction and Carlisle there are no less than twenty-two viaducts and fourteen tunnels. The summit of the line is at Ais Gill, 1,169 feet above sea level. Up to 7,000 navvies were employed and the line took seven years to build, finally opening on 1 May 1876. One of the most impressive structures is the 440-yard-long Batty Moss (Ribblehead) viaduct. On a gloomy winter day in 1988 Class 47 No. 47588 heads across the viaduct with a diverted WCML service. In the background is the imposing mass of Ingleborough.

In the winter of 1895 most stations on the line had a service of four or five trains day. Kirkby Stephen only had three but with additional stops on 'cattle sale days'. There were three London Scotland services, the fastest taking 6 hours 40 minutes to Carlisle. There was also a nightly sleeper. By the summer of 1953 things had not improved, rather the reverse in fact. The fastest London train, the Thames–Clyde Express, took 6 hours 55 minutes to Carlisle, while the local stations now had a service of just three or four trains daily. Appleby had a better service and most through trains from London, Manchester, Leeds and Derby called there. In the early 1980s the Nottingham to Glasgow services were diverted away from the S&C and replaced by a Leeds to Carlisle service. On 22 September 1990 No. 47459 rolls into Garsdale with the 15.16 Carlisle to Leeds.

A view from the other platform shows the Grade II listed signal box. The box is a Midland type 4c of 1910. It is listed for an unusual reason. Six months after it came into operation an error by the signalman led to a Scotch express running into the back of two light engines. In the resulting accident twelve people were killed. This disaster led to the widespread introduction of track circuiting. In the background is the twelve-arch Dandry Mire viaduct.

A few stations closed in the 1940s and 1950s but then in 1970 all stations between Settle Junction and Carlisle, apart from Settle and Appleby, were closed. In fact there was a proposal to withdraw all passenger services leaving just two long sidings to service mineral workings at each end of the line. However, the line came into its own as a diversionary route while electrification of the WCML was taking place in the early 1970s. In the summer of 1975 at weekends the popular Dalesrail service started and Horton-in-Ribblesdale, Ribblehead, Dent and Garsdale stations were reopened for the benefit of ramblers. This service continued and was extended in subsequent years. In 1980 the Cumbrian Mountain Pullman steam-hauled service started running. On 27 November 1982 Maunsell 4-6-0 No. 850 *Lord Nelson* passes through Dent station with the northbound Cumbrian Mountain Pullman. (Photo: David Ingham)

In the early 1980s the government minister responsible stated that he was minded to close the line. A vigorous public campaign led by the Friends of the Settle Carlisle Line, aided by the fact that many people wanted to have a last ride on the doomed line led to a massive increase in ridership. Ron Cotton, the BR manager given the responsibility of closing the line, in fact reopened a number of stations, leading to a further increase in use. Finally in 1989 it was announced that the line would not close. Since that time the S&C has gone from strength to strength – ridership having risen from 90,000 in 1983 to 1.2 million in 2012. The 78-mile-long line is now a conservation area. Several stations have protected status, including Appleby, seen here, which is Grade II listed. On 11 March 1989 Class 47 No. 47488 *Rail Riders* stand at the platform with the 12.42 Carlisle to Leeds.

On the same day Class 47 No. 47527 *Kettering* approaches the station with the diverted 10.25 Glasgow to Euston. The subsidiary signal is for the Warcop branch, the junction for which is behind the train. This was the last remnant of the Eden Valley Railway (see map on page 55).

On 4 March 1989 at Horton-in-Ribblesdale Class 47 No. 47441 passes through with the diverted 06.52 Aberdeen to Penzance. The buildings along the S&C were all designed by John Holloway Sanders. All are single storey buildings of a similar style. Horton was one of the stations reopened in 1986.

Another reopened station is Kirkby Stephen, previously Kirkby Stephen West, named as such to distinguish it from the NER station of Kirkby Stephen East. The popularity of the line with ramblers is evident in this 11 March 1989 view as the Leeds train arrives for the homeward journey.

In 2003/4 Arriva, the franchisee for the line, hired in a number of Mk2 carriages and Class 37 locomotives from EWS to provide additional capacity. On 2 March 2004 Class 37s Nos 37405 and 37411 top and tail the 13.33 Carlisle to Leeds at Kirkby Stephen. The station buildings are today leased by the Settle & Carlisle Railway Trust and include rentable holiday accommodation.

On the same day Class 60 No. 60034 *Carnedd Llewelyn* approaches the station with 6M52, the 10.16 Drax to Newbiggin gypsum train.

South of New Biggin is Culgaith. The station here opened in 1880 and closed along with the others in 1970. On 11 March 1989 Class 47 No. 47532 *Blue Peter* approaches the station with the diverted 11.14 Manchester Victoria to Glasgow.

The S&C has proved extremely popular for steam-hauled railtours. On 22 September 1990 Gresley V2 2-6-2 No. 4771 *Green Arrow* attacks the 1 in 100 at Smardale on the southbound leg of the Cumbrian Mountain Express.

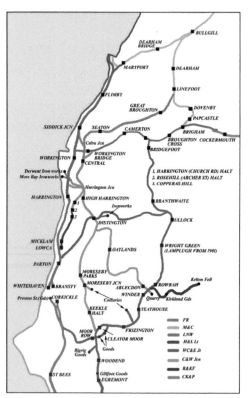

The railways of West Cumbria.

The London & North Western Railway In West Cumbria

The Whitehaven Junction Railway

With the railway between Maryport and Carlisle due to be completed in 1845, it would leave the maritime towns of Workington and Whitehaven at a disadvantage, so it was no surprise when a bill was put before Parliament in 1844 proposing a line between Maryport, Workington and Whitehaven. The chairman of the Whitehaven Junction Railway was Lord Lonsdale and the engineer George Stephenson. The Act was received on the 30 June 1844 and work on the 11-mile seventy-two chains line was completed by 19 March 1847. There were stations at Flimby, Workington Main, Harrington, Parton and Whitehaven Bransty. Authorisation for an extension to Whitehaven Harbour was received in 1848. At Whitehaven in 1954 Stanier 4MT 2-6-4T No. 42429 waits to leave with a service to Carlisle. (Photo: Walter Dendy)

On 2 June 1990 a Class 108 arrives at Whitehaven with the 09.10 Newcastle to Barrow. Bransty signal box is in the background.

A Class 142 'Pacer' departs from Parton with a southbound service on 21 April 1995.

A joint LNW/Cleator and Workington station was opened at Siddick Junction in 1880. This was primarily an exchange station between the two railways. It closed on 1 October 1934. FR 'Cleator Tank' 0-6-2T No. 98 of 1904 is seen at Siddick Junction with a passenger train.

Workington station in 1990. The middle roads have since been disconnected. In the distance is Workington Main No. 3 signal box. A Class 31 locomotive lurks in one of the bays.

Workington loco shed opened in 1876 originally with six roads. It was enlarged to twelve roads in 1890. This view dates from 1954. Among others in the line-up are a pair of Ivatt Class 4MT 2-6-0s, both single and double chimney versions, a pair of MR 4F 0-6-0s, and an MR 'Jinty' 3F 0-6-0T. (Photo: Walter Dendy)

On 13 August 1951 Webb 'Cauiliflower' 2F 0-6-0 No. 58396 is seen at Workington shed. Prior to Nationalisation these engines were the main motive power on the CK&P. In 1951 Workington had an allocation of four of these machines. (Photo: Ben Brooksbank)

In 1968 Workington closed as a steam depot but continued to house diesels. Later it was used for wagon repairs and maintenance as seen in this 1990 view.

The Cockermouth & Workington Railway

The Act for the C&W was passed on 21 July 1845. The first sod was turned on 8 February 1846 and the 8.5-mile single track opened on 27 April 1847. On opening there were just two intermediate stations, at Brigham and Camerton, joined shortly after by Workington Bridge. The initial passenger service was of four return services per day. From 1858 trains ran through from Cockermouth to both Carlisle and to Whitehaven. Broughton Cross Station had long since closed when this photograph was taken in 1961. (Photo: Ben Brooksbank)

The railway went through troubled times. Income from the transport of coal, the principal traffic, was much less than expected. The permanent way and rolling stock fell into disrepair. Matters started to improve towards the end of the decade and in to the 1860s. With the opening of the CK&P in 1865 a new joint station was built at Cockermouth, the old one becoming the goods depot. Passenger services were now integrated with the CK&P. In 1866 the C&W was leased by the LNW, which at the same time leased the WJR. In that same year a junction was made with the WC&E's Marron extension. A new station was opened at Marron Junction, which closed to passenger traffic as early as 1897. Broughton Cross closed on 2 March 1942, Workington Bridge in 1951, and Camerton the year after. Brigham survived until the line closed completely in 1966. This is a view towards Cockermouth at Brigham station in September 1961. (Photo: Ben Brooksbank)

The Whitehaven, Cleator & Egremont Railway

The WC&E was a response to the need to transport the huge quantities of iron ore, as well as coal and limestone, that were starting to be mined in the area. The first section, opened in 1856, was from Mirehouse Junction, on the W&FJ, to Moor Row and Egremont, with branches to Frizington and Cleator Moor, the location of the Whitehaven Iron & Steel Company. Around Moor Row and Cleator branches sprang out in all directions to service the various mines and quarries in the area. In June 1861 authorisation was received to extend northwards to Kidburngill, and a further 6.5-mile extension to meet the C&W line north of Bridgefoot was opened in 1866. Mirehouse Junction to Moor Row was doubled in 1863 and the line to Marron Junction followed in stages, being completed by 1873. This is Moor Row station in 1952 looking east. (Photo: Walter Dendy)

Another view at Moor Row looking east. The lines curving away to the right behind the signal box are to Egremont and Sellafield. (Photo: Walter Dendy)

Congestion at Whitehaven led the WC&E to propose extending the line from Egremont to Sellafield. At first bitterly opposed by the W&FJ, an agreement was eventually reached to operate the line jointly. The company was highly profitable. In the fifteen years from 1860 it had paid an average dividend of 10.75 per cent. Overtures from other companies were resisted until finally in 1878 when the WC&E became jointly owned by the FR and LNW. Before this event the railway had obtained powers to build a line from Ullock to the Gilgarran colliery. These powers were later extended to enable the building of a line through to Distington and thence to Parton. Opening took place on 23 October 1879. The long closed Beckermet station is seen in September 1961. (Photo: Ben Brooksbank)

Between Mirehouse Junction and Sellafield there were stations at Moor Row, Woodend, Egremont and Beckermet, and between Moor Row and Marron Junction at Cleator, Frizington, Yeathouse, Rowrah, Wright Green (later renamed Lamplugh), Ullock, Branthwaite and Bridgefoot. Gradients were fierce. On the Mirehouse Junction to Moor Row section there gradients were as steep as 1 in 52, and between Rorah and Marron up to 1 in 44. A gradient post is seen here near Moor Row showing 1 in 72.

From the late nineteenth century onwards the railway, along with the rest of the network in West Cumberland, went into s slow decline. Ullock Junction to Distington closed completely in 1929. Passenger services, which were never as important at freight traffic, were withdrawn between Rowrah and Marron Junction in 1931, and from Whitehaven and Sellafield in 1935, although briefly restored between 1946 and 1947. Rowrah to Marron closed to freight on 3 May 1954 and Beckermet to Sellafield on 18 January 1970. Moor Row to Rowrah was out of use by 1978 and Moor Row to Beckermet by 1980. A single track remained between Mirehouse Junction and Moor Row until *c.* 1990. Moor Row station is seen here on 1 June 1990.

The platforms and goods shed at Egremont in June 1990. Now demolished.

The crossing gates at Woodend, seen in 1990, together with an LNW/FR boundary marker.

The Cleator & Workington Junction Railway

The creation of the Cleator & Workington Junction Railway came about as a reaction to the high freight tariffs being charged by the LNW and WC&E for transporting the huge quantities of ore, coal, limestone and pig iron needed in the smelting industry. Matters came to a head after an increase in charges by both companies in 1873. The ironmasters, supported by local landowners, proposed an independent railway from Cleator Moor to Workington and on to Maryport. Despite opposition from the LNW and WC&E the authorising Act was passed on 27 June 1876. Before the main line of the C&WJ had been completed a further Act authorised a line from Distington to Rowrah. This line would link up with the Rowrah & Kelton Fell Mineral Railway. Workington central station seen in May 1951. This was also the headquarters of the C&WJ. (Photo: Walter Dendy)

The Cleator Moor–Workington–Siddick Junction line opened to mineral traffic on 1 July 1878, and to passenger traffic in the following October. At the same time branches to the Derwent Ironworks and to Harrington Rosehill came into use. On the 'main line' there were stations at Cleator Moor, Keekle Halt, Moresby Junction Halt, Moresby Parks, Distington, High Harrington and Workington Central. The total length from Cleator Moor to Siddick Junction was just over 11.25 miles. The line rose steeply towards Moresby Parks, mostly at 1 in 70/72, and fell equally steeply to Workington. This view looks north at Harrington Junction in April 1951. The Moss Bay and Derwent lines curve away to the left. (Photo: Walter Dendy)

The 6.5-mile Rowrah line opened in May 1882 and in the same year a branch to the Workington Iron Works was opened. Here gradients were even steeper, with over 2 miles at 1 in 44 from Rowrah Branch Junction to near Oatlands station. The Moss Bay branch and the Harrington Harbour branches opened in 1885 and 1893 respectively. The northern extension line was originally intended to join the M&C line at Dearham. Following discussions with that company the junction with the M&C was made at Linefoot on the Derwent branch. This 6.33-mile line opened in 1887. There were stations at Seaton, Camerton Colliery Halt and Great Broughton. Seaton station closed to passengers as early as 1922. The gradient here changes from 1 in 70 to 1 in 150. (Photo: Walter Dendy)

From the outset the 'main line' and the northern extension were worked by the Furness Railway. The transport of passengers on the system was very much a secondary consideration. The initial service provided was of three return services a day between Cleator Moor and Siddick Junction. By 1895 this had grown to four but by then on the northern extension there was just a Saturdays only service between Workington and Seaton. Mineral traffic on the Rowrah branch was hauled by the company's own locomotives. Distington was the meeting point of the WC&E and C&WJ systems. The line to the left is the branch to Ullock, while straight ahead leads to Moor Row. (Photo: Walter Dendy)

The best years for the railway were those preceding the First World War. In the record year of 1909 1,600,000 tons of minerals were carried. The C&WJ ended its independent existence at the 1923 Grouping, when it became part of the LMS. Before that, since the end of the First World War the railway had been in slow decline. Remaining passenger services were terminated in 1931 and the network closed section by section as ironworks, collieries and mines ceased production. The Rowrah line closed entirely in 1938. The last remaining vestige of the system was the line from Siddick Junction to Broughton Moor via Calva Junction. This closed in 1992. Looking north at Calva Junction. The lines on the left lead to Siddick Junction; those on the right to Seaton. (Photo: Walter Dendy)

The majority of the C&WJ system was worked by the FR. However, for the mineral lines the company used its own locomotives. All but one were saddle tanks and all were named after the homes of the directors of the company. Robert Stephenson & Co. 0-6-0ST No. 3 *South Lodge* was built in 1884 and continued to work until 1920.

The 3.5-mile-long Rowrah & Kelton Fell Mineral Railway was constructed in 1877 to transport iron ore and limestone. Until the Rowrah branch of the C&WJ was completed traffic was taken forward by the WC&E. Once the former was completed traffic switched to that line. Traffic on the line was worked by the company's own locomotive, a Neilson & Co. 0-4-0 *Kelton Fell* of 1876. When this locomotive was moved away in 1914 it is likely that the line was worked by C&WJ engines. *Kelton Fell* ended up working for the National Coal Board at Gartshore Colliery and was subsequently preserved by the Scottish Railway Preservation Society, where it is seen at Bo'ness. (Photo: David Ward)

The Lowca Light Railway

The 2-mile-long Lowca Light Railway, owned by the Workington Iron & Steel Company, was built partly on an ancient wagonway, which dated back to 1760. It ran from Lowca to Rosehill Junction where it made an end-on connection with a branch from Harrington junction. The railway connected the collieries and by-product plant at Lowca, and the brickworks at Micklam with the blast furnaces at Workington. Gradients were extreme, being as steep as 1 in 17. Unsurprisingly banking of trains was the norm. A workmen's passenger service between Workington and Lowca started on 15 April 1912, to be followed by the inauguration of a public service between Seaton and Lowca on 2 June the following year. Intermediate stations were Workington, Rosehill, Copperas Hill, and Micklam. In 1918 an additional stop was added at Harrington Church Road. The passenger service ceased in 1926 but the line continued to fulfil its main purpose of carrying freight until 1973. FR Sharp Stewart 0-6-0 No. 92 prepares to leave Lowca on the first day of the public service to Workington on 2 June 1913.

The Caledonian Railway In Cumbria

The Caledonian Railway main line between Carlisle and Beattock was completed in 1847. In England there were stations at Gretna, Floriston and Rockcliffe. Floriston closed in 1950 and Gretna in 1951. Rockcliffe closed briefly during the First World War and the passenger service was finally withdrawn in 1950. This was not quite the end of things as workmen's trains continued to run for the benefit of workers at the nearby marshalling yard. In the years before the First World War a McIntosh 'Dunalastair' 4-4-0 departs from Rockcliffe with a local service to Carlisle.

The Solway Junction Railway

Solway Viaduct at Bowness-on-Solway

The impetus for the building of the Solway Junction Railway came from a wish to avoid the lengthy and expensive journey via Carlisle for the ore that was being shipped from West Cumbria to the ironworks in Ayrshire and Lanarkshire. The SJR received its Act on 30 June 1864 but the route of the line was not finally decided until the Solway Junction Act of 1867. The company was authorised to build a line from Kirtlebridge on the Caledonian main line to Kirkbride Junction on the North British Silloth branch, and a line from Abbey Junction to Brayton Junction on the Maryport and Carlisle main line. These plans would require the building of a viaduct across the Solway larger than any yet built. The total length of these two lines was 21.75 miles, which included the 1,940-yard viaduct.

Goods traffic started on 13 September 1869 and passenger traffic between Kirtlebridge and Bowness on 8 March 1870. The line was opened fully to Brayton Junction on 28 July 1870. There were stations at Annan (Annan Shawhill from 1924), Bowness, Whitrigg, Abbey Junction, and Broomfield (opened on 1 April 1873, renamed Bromfield on 1 November 1895). Soon in trouble, in 1873 the SJR sold the Kirtlebridge to Annan line to the CR for £84,439. The CR worked the line from the outset and took over the SJR completely in 1895. In that year there were four services daily between Kirtlebridge and Brayton plus one train between Kirtlebridge and Annan only. In LMS days a CR Lambie 4-4-0T stands at Annan Shawhill with a single carriage.

In 1881 the viaduct suffered severe damage from ice floes on the Solway. It was repaired and reopened in 1885. By 1921 it was in poor condition and closed for repairs. This marked the end of passenger services on the English side. The repairs were never carried out and the viaduct was dismantled in 1933. In the same year the Abbey Junction to Brayton Junction line closed. Bromfield, seen here, was the only station on this line.

Bowness-on-Solway station closed along with the viaduct in 1921. This is the view looking south. The station staff seem to have gone to a lot of trouble to make their station look attractive.

A view taken in the other direction, towards the viaduct. Note the very typical Caledonian Railway signal box.

Another CR signal box is seen at Brayton Junction, where the SJR joined the M&C main line. The SJR branch is the line curving away to the left.

The SJR had a fleet of six locomotives: Nos 1 and 2 were 0-4-2 well tanks, Nos 3 and 4 were 0-4-2 tender engines, and Nos 5 and 6 were 0-6-0 tender engines. All were built by Neilson & Co. Dating from 1868, Nos 5 and 6 were originally intended for the London, Chatham & Dover Railway. They survived into LMS ownership where they received the numbers 17101 and 17102, being finally withdrawn in 1927/28. No. 17102 is depicted in LMS days. Notice the unusually spoked driving wheels.

The North British
Railway In Cumbria

Port Carlisle and Silloth

In 1823 the Carlisle Canal opened between Carlisle and Fisher's Cross, later renamed Port Carlisle. Initially profitable, by the middle of the century competition from local railways, particularly the Maryport & Carlisle, had led to much diminished returns and thoughts turned to converting the canal into a railway. The authorising Act for the Port Carlisle Dock & Railway Company was passed on 4 August 1853 and the railway was completed the following year, opening for goods in May and for passengers in the following month. The terminus of this single track line was at the canal basin in Carlisle. There were stations at Burgh, later renamed Burgh by Sands, Kirkandrews, and Glasson. The Newcastle & Carlisle, which had opened a branch to the canal basin in 1837, worked the line until the PCD&R purchased its own engines. In 1857 as an economy measure passenger traffic became horse drawn. This is the era of the famous 'Dandy'. There were various Dandies over the years, one of which, Dandy No. 1, is now preserved in the National Railway Museum.

Goods traffic continued to be steam hauled until 1899 when due to the poor state of the track this too became horse drawn. In 1914 the track was upgraded and steam haulage was put in place for both kinds of traffic. On 31 May 1932 all traffic ceased and the line was abandoned. The specially adorned train inaugurated the return of steam-hauled services on 4 April 1914. The locomotive is NBR Class R (LNER Class J82) 0-6-0T No. 22.

Even before the canal had been converted to a railway the directors of the company were thinking about an extension to Silloth where a new dock would be constructed. This 13-mile line was authorised by the Carlisle & Silloth Bay Railway & Dock Company Act of 16 July 1855. Construction was rapid and the railway opened in August the following year. In 1857 the stations of Kirkbride, Abbey and Black Dyke were opened. Rolling stock was supplied by the North British Railway, which leased both the PCD&R and C&SBR&D from 1861. The new dock was completed in 1859. Black Dyke station seems far from any settlement. (Photo: Ben Brooksbank)

The C&SBR&D bought up land at Silloth, which it tried to develop as a resort. The town and railway gained further impetus with the opening of the Border Union Railway in 1864 and promotion by the NBR. In 1880 the two companies were amalgamated with the NBR and from 1 July trains started to run into Carlisle Citadel. In 1863 a branch was constructed to reach a platform at the Silloth Sanatorium. This line left the main line to the east of Silloth station. A further branch leading off this branch led to a firing range for testing small calibre armament. This was built in 1886. The sanatorium is seen with a special train at its platform.

Silloth Port was extremely busy during the Second World War but decline set in thereafter. In the last summer of steam operation of passenger services there were five return trips daily plus an additional Monday and Thursday service non-stop between Carlisle and Silloth. Saturdays saw an additional three trains. There were three services on Sundays. The following year diesel multiple units were introduced on the line, which was still seeing substantial numbers of passengers at holiday times. Despite this the line was slated for closure in the Beeching Report and did so on 7 September 1964. The last train was the 7.58 p.m. from Silloth to Carlisle hauled by Ivatt 4MT 2-6-0 No. 43139. Standing at the head of the 14.20 to Carlisle on 6 August 1951 is Reid J35 0-6-0 No. 64478. (Photo: Walter Dendy)

The Waverley Route

The NBR Waverley route in England owed its origin to the Border Union (North British) Railway Act of 21 July 1859, which authorised a line 43 miles in length from Hawick to Carlisle, the section from Edinburgh to Hawick having been completed by 1849. The Act included a junction with the Carlisle & Silloth Bay Railway at Rattlingate. The line opened throughout to passengers on 1 July 1862. However, before then a service had operated between Carlisle and Scotch Dyke from 29 October 1861. The Langholm branch was opened on 18 April 1864. There was also a branch from Longtown to Gretna where the Caledonian main line was joined. In England there were stations at Kershopefoot, Penton, Riddings, the junction for Langholm, Scotch Dyke, Longtown, Lyneside and Harker. This is a view of Kershopefoot station from the interwar years.

Never an outstanding success the line gained considerably in importance in 1876 when the Midland Railway, having completed the Settle & Carlisle line, used the Waverley route to reach Edinburgh. In 1895 the MR was running three services daily from St Pancras to Edinburgh, one of these a sleeper, which made the journey in just 9.5 hours. In 1922 there were five expresses running between Carlisle and Edinburgh plus two stopping trains, Carlisle to Langholm and Carlisle to Hawick. Probably the most famous train to traverse the route was the Thames–Forth Express. This began running in 1927, lost its name during the Second World War but continued unnamed thereafter. In 1953 it left St Pancras daily at 9.00 a.m. and arrived in Edinburgh at 7.14 p.m. It will be noted that this is a slower time than in 1895! It gained the name The Waverley and continued until 1964. At Carlisle on 11 August 1960 North British J35 No. 64608 is in charge of the 18.13 stopping train to Hawick, where it will arrive at 19.47. (Photo: Ben Brooksbank)

By the early 1960s the writing was on the wall for the Waverley route. The Beeching Report in 1963 had drawn attention to the fact that there were less than 5,000 passengers per week in the southern part of the line. Despite a vigorous anti-closure campaign the whole line closed on 6 January 1969. Longtown station closed with the rest of the line in 1969 but the line here remained open until 1970 for goods traffic to the army depot.

The Langholm Branch had closed in 1964, with the junction station of Riddings closing at the same time. In September 1962 Ivatt 4MT 2-6-0 No. 43045 waits to leave Langholm with a service for Carlisle. (Photo: Lamberhurst)

Classmate No. 43049 is seen crossing the Caledonian main lines just north of Carlisle as it heads north on the Waverley route with a mixed freight on 7 May 1965. (Photo: Ben Brooksbank)

The South Durham & Lancashire Union Railway

The Stockton & Darlington Railway had reached Barnard Castle by 1856. Backed by the S&D the SD&LUR was authorised in 1857 to extend the railway to Tebay on the west coast line. The line, which was completed in 1861, presented some formidable engineering challenges, including the 1,040-feet-long Belah Viaduct designed by Thomas Bouch, the engineer for the line. There were gradients of up to 1 in 59 for westbound trains and 1 in 72 for those travelling east. Stations in Cumbria were Barras, Kirkby Stephen, Ravenstonedale, and Gaisgill. In 1862 the SD&LU was taken over by the S&D, which was itself absorbed by the NER the following year. The initial passenger service was of two trains each way daily but there were many more goods and mineral trains. The main motive behind the line's construction was the transport of iron ore eastwards and coal and coke westwards. In 1895 there was a service of five trains daily between Darlington and Tebay plus a service between Kirkby Stephen and Tebay. Journey time between Darlington and Tebay was 1 hour 50 minutes to 2 hours. The western end of the line saw no trains on Sundays. Ravenstonedale (Newbiggin until 1877) closed to passenger traffic on 1 December 1952.

An NER '910' class 2-4-0 No. 126 is seen at Gaisgill with a train of six-wheeled carriages. Gaisgill also closed in 1952 but the line remained in use for freight traffic until 1962.

Between Smardale and Ravenstonedale is the 550-feet-long Smardalegill Viaduct, which crosses Scandal Beck. It is listed Grade II*.

Part of the former SD&LUR trackbed, including the viaduct, has been made into a public footpath. This is the point where the path passes through the Smardale Viaduct of the Settle & Carlisle line.

The extensive layout at Kirkby Stephen, *c.* 1910. The area this side of the bridge, including the goods shed, is now a campsite. The locomotive is a '1001' class 0-6-0, a type which originated with the S&D and was extensively used on the SD&LUR and the Eden Valley Railway.

In the interwar years Ivatt D3 4-4-0 No. 4346 waits to depart from Kirkby Stephen with a westbound service.

The Stainmore Railway was established in 2000 in the former Kirkby Stephen East station. They currently have a 0.33-mile running line and their eventual ambition is to link up with the Eden Valley Railway at Warcop. This view shows the rather lopsided appearance of Kirkby Stephen station today.

The Eden Valley Railway

On 21 May 1858 the Eden Valley Railway was authorised to build a line from Kirkby Stephen to Eden Valley Junction, just south of Penrith on the west coast line. The line opened in 1862 and was worked from the outset by the S&D. There were stations at Musgrave, Warcop, Appleby (from 1850 Appleby East), Kirkby Thore, Temple Sowerby, Clifton (from 1927 Clifton Moor) and Cliburn. There was a connection with the S&C at the north end of Appleby (MR) station. Cliburn station is seen following closure.

In 1947 there was a service of three trains daily between Darlington and Penrith with a service of just two trains between Kirkby Stephen and Tebay. On this latter section passenger services were withdrawn in 1952. Services between Barnard Castle and Penrith succumbed ten years later. The line between Kirkby Stephen and Appleby (LMR) was retained for stone traffic and after this ceased, the section north of Warcop continued to see occasional use by the army. After 1989 the line was redundant but in 1995 the Eden Valley Railway Society was set up and in 2006 ran its first trains. Appleby station is seen *c.* 1900 with a Class '1001' 0-6-0 at the head of a northbound service.

The Cockermouth, Keswick & Penrith Railway

The opening of the South Durham & Lancashire Union Railway gave impetus to the idea of a line from Penrith across to West Cumbria, the transport of coking coal westwards and iron ore eastwards being conceived as its main purpose. The Cockermouth, Keswick & Penrith Railway was authorised by an Act of 1 August 1861. The engineer for the 31.25-mile line was Thomas Bouch. The line, with no less than 135 bridges, was opened for mineral traffic on 26 October 1864 and for passenger traffic on 2 January 1865. There was an initial service of three trains daily in each direction. There were station at Blencow, Troutbeck, Penruddock, Threlkeld, Keswick, Braithwaite, Bassenthwaite Lake, Embleton and Cockermouth. At the latter location a new station joint with the Cockermouth & Workington was built, the old C&W station becoming a goods depot. The photo shows the view from the footplate of Ivatt 2MT 2-6-0 No.46491 as it approaches Cockermouth station with a Workington to Penrith train. Standing waiting to occupy the single track section is another locomotive of the same class. (Photo: Walter Dendy)

There was a halt at Low Briery, east of Keswick, in use for workers at a bobbin mill until closure in 1958, and another at Highgate, west of Troutbeck, used by schoolchildren between 1908 and 1928. There were severe gradients on the eastern half of the line. Almost immediately after leaving Penrith trains had to climb at 1 in 79/70 for some 4 miles, and in the opposite direction, from Troutbeck to Threlkeld at 1 in 62.5. At Bassenthwaite Ivatt 2MT 2-6-0 No. 46449 stands at the head of the 10.15 SO Manchester Victoria to Workington. (Photo: Ben Brooksbank)

An Act of 29 June 1863 provided for the LNW to work all traffic except mineral, which was to be worked by the Stockton & Darlington, which now owned the SD&LUR and the Eden Valley Railway. The Red Hills Curve, between Eamont Junction on the EVR and Redhills Junction on the CK&P, was brought into use on 5 September 1866, henceforth obviating the need for reversal at Penrith. The NER, by now having absorbed the S&D, worked mineral trains through to Cockermouth. As the century progressed, coking coal now being found locally and iron ore similarly, being used in the furnaces of West Cumbria, mineral traffic declined and the line started to become more dependent on tourist traffic. To cope with this increasing traffic the line between Penrith and Threlkeld was doubled in 1901. The locomotive seen at the Up platform at Keswick is Webb 2-4-0 'Precedent' class No. 1675 *Vimiera*.

Probably the most famous train to traverse the line was The Lakes Express. This started running in 1922, though was only named as such from 1927. After a break during the Second World War it continued until 1965. In the summer of 1953 the train left Euston every weekday at 11.50 a.m. and arrived at Oxenholme at 5.22 p.m. where it divided, one part going to Windermere, arrival 6.50 p.m., the other going through to Workington, arrival 8.45 p.m. In the same period on Saturdays there were through services from Liverpool Exchange and Manchester Victoria. Other than these there were four return services daily traversing the line. There was no Sunday service. In January 1955 diesel multiple units were introduced to the line. This led to the resumption of Sunday services and the reopening of Blencow station, which had been closed since 1952. Through goods traffic ceased on 1 June 1964 and the line west of Keswick was closed on 18 April 1966. Just over two weeks before that date, on 2 April, the Lakes and Fells Railtour took place. Ivatt 2MT 2-6-0s Nos 46458 and 46426 stand at Keswick en route to Workington. (Photo: J. W. Sutherland)

From 1 July the line from Penrith to Keswick effectively became a single track siding. Passenger services were finally withdrawn on 6 March 1972. Mineral trains to Flusco Quarry, west of Blencow, continued for a few more months. In August 1967 a Derby Lightweight unit stands at Keswick being loaded with mail before returning to Penrith. (Photo: Geoffrey Skelsey)